Title of Your Sex Tape

Jennifer Sinclair

POEMS FROM THE NINE-NINE

To all the Brooklyn 99 fans,
To all the poetry lovers,
To all the Boyle cousins –
I love you.

From the Author

Poems from the Nine-Nine is simply a series of quotes from the beloved television series. However, they are set out in a similar way to how the basic and popular poetry collection layout currently is.

With one-hundred and fifty poems, this book takes a spin on what modern poetry collections look like, without insulting or undermining these poets work. Call it a compliment, call it comedic, however you want to view it is the right way to view it.

The show currently has seven seasons out and some of the best quotes directly from these episodes are included. It's something to treasure, something to enjoy, and something to have a laugh at with the possibility of it motivating and inspiring you like modern poetry does today. Nine-Nine!

I hate when he says that. He should say "Cheers to the Ninety-Ninth precinct"

I'm so confused,
I don't know
What's happening right now.
- *Title of your Sex Tape*

Being able to read
Jake's handwriting is a gift.
A useless,
Useless gift.

It's the most fun day of the year.
Something you wouldn't understand
Because you're not programmed to feel joy.

Yes,
But my software is due
For an exuberance upgrade.

We could dance.
You must know some moves.
You were mentioned by name
In the "Monster Mash".

Wait a minute

This isn't the championship cummerbund.
This is some common cummerbund.
And you're not cheddar.
You're just some common bitch.

My nana always said,
"Bad news first
Because the good news is probably a lie."
Fun fact: she made me cry a lot.

We all have fears.
I'm so claustrophobic,
I can't even go into the
Downstairs supply closet.
I hear they have some hot new binder clips,
But I'll never know.

I love being Scary Terry.
He says what regular Terry's thinking.
This is taking too long!
I'm gonna miss the farmer's market!

The English Language
Cannot fully capture the depth
And complexity of my thoughts.
So, I'm incorporating emojis
Into my speech
To better express myself.
Winky face.

Hello, unsolved case.
Do you bring me joy?
No, because you're boring
And you're too hard.

See ya.

The human form
Of the 100 emoji.

I wasn't hurt that badly.
The doctor said
All my bleeding was internal.
That's where the blood's supposed to be.

True strength
Comes from
The pelvis.
Not the mouth.

Okay,
No hard feelings,
But I hate you.
Not joking.
      - *Bye.*

I ate one string bean.
It tasted like fish vomit.
That was it for me.

There is a bomb
At this wedding.
Your butt.
Your butt is the bomb.

I know how to kiss!
I've read books!

How was I
Supposed to know
There'd be consequences
For my actions?

With all due respect,
I am gonna
Completely ignore
Everything you just said.

Turn your greatest weakness
Into your greatest strength.
Like Paris Hilton,
RE: her sex tape.

It's such a classic Boyle trait
To not recognize talent.
My cousin Susan didn't know she could sing
Until her late forties.

Jennifer Sinclair

I'd like your eight-dollarest
Bottle of wine, please.

All men
Are at least 30% attracted to me.
My mother cried
The day I was born,
Because she knew
She would never be better than me.
At any given moment,
I'm thinking about one thing:
Richard Dreyfuss hunkered over eating dog
food.
I feel like
I'm the Paris of people.

Have you seen
Captain Holt?
Tall, handsome gentleman
Dressed like an airline pilot.

Okay, let's talk about planets.
Jupiter is a gas giant.
So's Hitchcock. How does this help me?

Wuntchtime is over.
Boom! Did it.
Had it both ways.
No regrets.

You all right, Captain? Tough weekend?
I went to Barbados with my husband.
We wove hats out of palm fronds
And swam with the stingrays.
I've never been happier.

I don't slump, people.
I opposite of slump.
I pmuls.
That's slump backwards
And it's what I do.
I pmuls all over this place.

There's a typo
In this crossword puzzle.

I passed
A slutty tree
On the way here.
Who wants
To have sex
With a tree?

Was it a maple?

H is for Holt.
He's leading us
Right to him.
Now, all we have to do
Is follow
The trail of chocolate.

This, this is why I became a cop.

That machine's
Been here forever.
It's basically
Part of the force.
Take Scully instead.
Yes, please.
Take me to the land
Of vending machines.

The toilet paper's
Only one ply now.
My butt hurts
All the time.
The AC is broken.
My butt hurts
All the time.
Scully's butt hurts
All the time.

Detectives,
Our monthly crime
Statistics are due.
I want all paperwork
On your closed cases
By tomorrow.
Scully,
You can just write
"I didn't close any"
On a piece of paper.

You've been needling
Poor Peralta so much,
You've practically made
Him a new suit.

"Needled him a new suit".
Even when we're fighting,
You're hilarious.
Stop it. Stop it.

Ghost Rider
And Ghost Rider Two.
Both mater-pie.

Great!
Who are we killing?
I won't do kids.
That's a rule.
But, that rule
Is negotiable
If the kid's
A dick.

I sold a guy
A fake Pekinese.
'Twas a cat.

You will not win
Me over with your use
Of 'twas.

'Twasn't trying to.

School is cool.
That's why it rhymes.

Whoa,
What happened?
You know what,
Forget it.
I'll just read
Amy's notes.

My back gave out
When I was dyeing
My pubes.
I was only halfway done.
I'm like Cruella de Vil
Down there.

What's his body like
On a scale of Charles to Terry.

Sorry, buddy,

What?
I'm the ten!

Sure you are.

He left a tiny crack
In the blind,
So I could read Captain's lips.
"Sharon and your kids
Will distract Jake.
They'll be here at nine-thirty sharp.
My waffle xylophone
On the cheese man."

My lip-reading is not flawless.

And when this is over,
I'm going to find you
And I'm going to break
Those little fingers.

Ms Diaz,
Please stop threatening
The stenographer.

You have all
Embarrassed the precinct.
Now when people
Think of the Nine-Nine,
They'll think of
Detective Diaz
Filling an iron
With tequila.

So I could make tequila steam.

Gina, since you're leaving,
I'd like to make a toast.
Bye.

Nikolaj.

55

If you fall down
Nine times,
You gotta reassess
Your walking
'Cause something's wrong.

Ames

I love you.
I love how smart you are.
I love how beautiful you are.
I love your face,
And I love your butt
I should've written this down first.

I can't take that.
It's clearly not cash,
And I don't have time
In my life to return things.

"Dear Captain Raymond Holt,
Thinking of you.
Best, Dr. Kevin Cozner, Ph.D."
They even used their pet names.

Jennifer Sinclair

Coat, coat, jacket, coat.
Is this a police precinct,
Or a Turkish bazaar?

Holt's Pants Were in That Bag

His knees
Are in the breeze.
He's in
His undies.

Hello
Raymond,
You're looking old,
And Sickly.

Do not trust
Any child that chews
Bubble-Flavored bubble gum.
Do not trust
Any adult
That chews gum at all.
Never vacation in
Banff.

Everything is garbage.
You find something you care about,
And it's taken from you.
Your colleagues,
Your dream job,
Your mango yogurt.
Never love anything.
That's the lesson.

Oh, you're right. I'm going to tell him.
It might not be today.
It might not be tomorrow.
It definitely won't be later than tomorrow.
So, pretty much today or tomorrow then.

The key with dogs
Is establishing the alpha.
Cheddar, drop it.
Please drop it.
It'll give you anything you want.

Oh, Cheddar is the alpha.
Didn't expect that.

Oh my god,
She's totally gonna flunk us.
I haven't gotten an F
Since I failed recess in second grade.

"Teachers need a break too, Amy."

I'm a detective.
I will detect.

Piece of advice:
Just give up.
It's the Boyle way.
That's why our family crest is a white flag.

The only thing
I'm not good at
Is modesty.
Because I'm great at it.

Jake, why don't you
Just do the right thing
And jump out of a window?

Captain Holt will never fire me
If he knows I'm mourning
The death of a close friend.

Actually,
Someone reported that
They couldn't find your head.
But we found it;
It was up your butt.
You're a fireman,
You should know
How to treat that burn.

It's a sloppy Jessica.
Mac n Cheese,
Chilli,
Pizza on a bun.
It's everything
I've wanted to each
For the last
Forty-eight hours.

Kwazy Cupcakes

It's so addictive, right?
I play so much that when I close my eyes at
night,
I just see cupcakes instead
Of my normal dizzying array of flashing
lights.

Why would you ever
Intentionally spill beans?
They're one of nature's most
Densely packed protein sources.

And they remain unsullied by flavor.

I really need that Gasinex.
I think there was
Some dairy in the cheesecake
That I ate for breakfast.

If anything goes wrong,
Scully, fake a heart attack.

What are you thinking?
Classic angina or
Something sexier
Like myocardial-infarction?

Just drop down
Onto the ground
And wiggle.

Hey Captain,
Something's going on
With this heist.
You tell us everything
You know,
And we'll tell you everything
We know.

I'd rather not.

Jokes on you,
We didn't know
Anything.

And Peralta,
I hope this will do.
It's a can
Of Orange Soda
From when
Some other
Children visited.

I've got a way
Better job now.
I'm working at one
Of those fancy
Hand Lotion Stores.
Spoiler alert:
I have a gun again,
And I've gotten to
Use it three times.
You would be surprised
How often teenage girls
Try and shoplift
Mango hand cream.

I'm working
On my vows.
What rhymes
With juicy heinie?

The Pontiac Bandit
And Jake the Cop.
Taking down crooks,
In the streets
Where they live.
Flirting with girls
Who are hot for the badge.
There's a talking police dog
That helps them solve crime.

Mangy Carl
Used to be a
Homeless gentleman.
I work with
A charity that finds
Jobs for down-on-their-luck
White people.

There's a triple-murderer
Loose in Brooklyn,
And it's our job
To bring him in.
Even if that means
Forgiving a guy
Who stole some cars,
And, yes, sold a few cats as dogs.

More than a few.
Weird how many people
Fell for that.

You've just lost
Rosa privileges.
From now on,
You can call me Diaz
Or Hey You.

But we have to let
The investigation run its course.
Right now,
Everyone's a suspect.
Except for Hitchcock and Scully.
Whoever did it
Took the stairs.

All Boyle men
Are blessed with a flat ass,
Which is perfect
For scooching.

Jennifer Sinclair

I felt like a superhero,
Like the Hulk's mom.

Well, there's no reason
To be defensive,
Just because you don't
Have the bone strength of a yogi.
We all have our thing.
You're a muscler,
I'm a boner.

"Bullets over Broadway"
was on TV.
And I came down with a
Big ol' Dianne Wiest infection

Like Yeast.

People think
If they put on a costume
They can just get away
With anything they want.
Halloween is Christmas
For jerks.

They'll deny everything.
We need hard proof.

So, let's get it.
Step one,
Put a delicious pie
In the fridge
And cover it with poison.

That's step one?
What's step two?

Tell their widows
They were thieves.

We could stop paying
For an exterminator.
It's pointless.
We all have guns.

Captain,
Hey!
Welcome,
To the murder.

Bingpot!

I remarked afterwards
That I wished the officiant
Had been more efficient.
It was very funny.
Kevin still talks about it.
Maybe I should open
With that zinger?

Hello Raymond

Surprised to see me?
Well, I didn't say
Bloody Mary Three times,
So yes.

When did she record this?
Judging by the flames
Around her,
It could be a livestream.

It's so hard to talk at work
Because there's no privacy.
The roof is freezing,
The holding cell is full of perps,
And their romantic advice is not great.
It's always to tell Vivian,
"Bitch, get your life right!"
I tried it.
She did not like it.

You're useless.
You are completely useless.
You are,
Without a doubt,
The most incompetent detectives
I've ever seen.
And I'm including the bomb sniffing dog
That humps all the bombs.

Ooh,
Mm-hmm,
Hmm-hmm-hmm,
Hmmmmm.

- *Marshed Mellow.*

I was thinking how I would make
The perfect American president,
Based upon my skill set,
Dance ability and bloodlust.

Why are you giving candy
To a baby
In the first place?
Don't give candy
To a baby!
They can't brush
Their teeth!

So, you choose your dad
Over me,
Your co-worker
Who hates you?

Hello,
You've reached the office
Of Raymond Holt.
I *can* come to the phone right now.

Do you know I love milk?
Well, I do,
But it hurts my stomach.
So, I haven't had milk,
A beverage I love,
For nineteen years.
Nineteen milkless years I've gone,
But for some reason, I can quit Kwazy
Cupcakes.

Scully, what's your basement like?
Bunch of old
Victorian wallpaper
That came with the house.
I tried to peel it off,
But the wall underneath
Was covered with fingernail scratches.

I met my wife
At an orgy.
Well, she was leaving
An orgy,
And we bumped
Into each other
On the street.
Real cute meet.

Wait,
I have a theory.
I think limousine
And magazine
Come from
The same word.

Hmm, yes.
I dread those
Enunciated denunciations.

Better get some
Corticosteroids to treat
That laryngeal fracture.
Sorry,
I couldn't bring myself
To call him a dirtbag.

And why would you?
A dirtbag
Is a very useful
Part of the vacuum cleaner.
Clearly,
It's a compliment.

All I know is,
I woke up
In a pool
Of my own blood
Next to a metal chair
That had a dent in it
The same shape
As my head.

What were you doing
Before the attack?

I was sitting
In said metal chair
Watching the season two
Premiere of The Masked Singer.
The Egg had just gone,
And I'm pretty sure
I know who it is:
Sara Gilbert.

The universe isn't gonna let
Anything happen to two
Best friends
Unless we're in a fiery crash,
And our bodies are burned
Beyond recognition.

I don't know
What I'm gonna do.
I guess
I could be a teacher.
"Sorry, Travis,
The answer's obviously Istanbul."
"What did you say to me?"
"No, maybe you're
Wasting your life."
"Sorry, Principal Ramos,
I didn't see you there."
"Wait, Travis
Is your son?"
"Hah, well,
I guess you're just
Gonna have to fire me."
"Fired? Me?
How dare you, sir."
"We will settle" –
See, it just wouldn't work.

It's just a windbreaker.
It's not like
I gave him a badge
And a gun…
Oh, he has
Both of those things.

Jake, help me.
I don't want to die.
I'm still on second season
Of Game of Thrones.

Doug Judy
Does not work
With Fire.

Yeah,
He's like the hound
From "Game of Thrones".

I am like the hound.
And you're
My Arya.

Blink twice
If you'd like me
To mercy kill you.

This is chaos.
Gina's been filing evidence
By perp hotness.

Fear is
A powerful aphrodisiac.

Sexy train
Is leaving the station.
Check out this caboose.
Later, sluts.

This is happening.
Jake and Amy
Are getting married tonight.
Title of *my* sex tape!

You just graduated
Pie school, bitches.
Sorry I said bitches,
I'm just really worked up.

Oh, God,
They're gonna shut this precinct down
And separate me and Jake.
Our friendship is over.
If he doesn't see my face every day,
He'll forget who I am.
He's like a goldfish.

Meat from the street.
Sounds like a fun treat.
Ha. I'm a poet and…
I didn't even know I was rhyming.

But it happened anyway.

It's not a fair fight.
Give the bird a gun,
Then see what happens.

I spent the whole night
Riding my bike,
Just thinking and riding,
Riding and thinking.
Also, I drank some water
From the stream.

Amy broke everything
And got us kicked out
Of the bar.
Then, we got attacked
By rats.

*It's the best
Thanksgiving ever.*

Captain Wuntch

Good to see you.
But if you're here,
Who's guarding hades?

By the power vested in me
By the state of New York,
I'd like to announce
That your honeymoon vacation request
Has officially been moved from pending
To approved.

Oh, I've caused a problem.
I think I am getting a text message.
Bloop.
Ah, there it is.

Honestly,
I'm going to last forever.
You hear that bitches?
I'm gonna last forever.

Turns out
I gave up easy.
You hear that bitches?
I gave up so easy.

My name is
Adelaide Van Hoyt.
I'm eight-nine years old,
And I'm here to report a crime.

Adelaide Van Hoyt.
Eight-nine years old.
Goatee, six three.
And two hundred and ninety pounds.

Hey!
This is a tight
Two-forty.
Show Adelaide some damn respect.

So nice of you to greet us,

Madeline.
I thought surely, you'd still be crushed
Under that house in Munchkinland.

There were two Kelly's.
You'd know that
If you'd ever listened
To my podcast.

Forget your sex
With meaningless sex.
It rhymes because it's true.

Now, for my first tweet,
I think I should give an update
On the water main break
That's actually informative.
"NYC H20-Main SITREP: at 2040 ED
Current PSI 456 MAX CAP 204000 LPM".
Suck on that tasty lemon drop,
Olivia Crawford.

I found my gun.
It was in my holster.
My holster's on my butt.

"Tie a yellow ribbon
Round the old oak tree,
'cause this boy's comin' home".

"Con Air".
What have I become?

I got shot down
Smuggling ammo
To a rebel group,
Flying an old
Soviet plan prop.
They tortured us.
Made me eat
My co-pilot's tongue.
Now, I've got a taste for it.

Oh, P.I., huh?
I like that.
"Hello, Mr. Branville,
I found out where your wife's
Been going tonight.
Have a seat,
You're not gonna like this.
She's cheating on you.
What do you mean
You knew that already?
You killed her?
And are framing me
For the murder?
I just left my prints
All over the crime scene.
Oh, you are an evil ge-".
This,
This I could get onboard for.

Jennifer Sinclair

New York's Finest
Just got a whole
Lot finer.

The thin blue line
Just got thick
As hell.

This place
Smells like a squid
Farted inside
A whale's butt.

He's messing with me
Because I'm not intimidating
Like Terry
Or dignified like Jake.
Or model-handsome like Jake.
Or funny like Jake.

We buried Nana Boyle
At the family farm,
But because of the soil's
High salt content,
She turned into jerky.

Sticks and Stones, Raymond
Describing your breakfast?

The hospital called.
Your test results came
Back positive.
You're a stage five dumbass.

I was working out
And I saw a muscle in my shoulder
I'd never seen before.

I thought
It might have been
A scientific discovery.

She's the devil.
And you don't dance with the devil
Because you get burned.

Also, because in Madeline's case,
She has no rhythm,
And her hands are like little rat claws.

He's crashing!
Push 10 ccs of corticosteroids,
Plus prep the ER
For surgical decompression!
I don't know what any of this means,
But I feel like Sandra Oh.

You should be very proud of yourself.
I know things aren't exactly
Where you want to be right now,
But,
I promise you they will improve.

Every time someone steps up
And says who they are,
The world becomes a better,
More interesting place.

So, thank you.